Postmodern and Youth Discipleship

Commitment or Looking Cool?

Graham Cray

Principal, Ridley Hall, Cambridge

GROVE BOOKS LIMITED
RIDLEY HALL RD CAMBRIDGE CB3 9HU

Contents

The Cover Illustration is by Peter Ashton

First Impression December 1998
ISSN 0144-171X
ISBN 1 85174 389 8

1

Young People in Their Contemporary Pastoral Context

'The life experience of young people in modern industrialized societies have changed quite significantly over the last two decades.'[1]

A highly experienced youth worker, who was also a youth work trainer, had worked relationally with a group of teenage girls at a school for a number of months. One morning she was dropped off at the school by a good looking male trainee. All the group of young women she had been working with could talk about was the appearance of her driver. It seemed to the worker that, despite her commitment to and skill at relational youth work, the young women were not looking for commitment, but were wholly focused on appearance and looking cool. The experience raised questions about what young people really wanted, what forces shaped their expectations of life, and what sort of work and pastoral care they need and would accept.

This booklet will focus on the social and cultural forces which shape young people's lives and expectations so as to identify crucial areas for pastoral ministry. The connection between lives and expectations is an important one as people's experience of life within a culture gives plausibility to certain explanations of it and understandings within it. As Andrew Walker has written, 'Ideas and world views are maintained by social support. They are culturally embedded in community.'[2] What young people regard as 'obvious,' as common sense about lifestyle and expectations, will relate to the primary forces which shape the society in which they live. 'The power of any culture is measured by the extent to which its formulations seem "natural."'[3] The overall power of a culture is such that 'youth culture' is only of secondary importance. It is the impact of the mainstream culture, not least changes in it, upon the life experience of young people that is most influential and which raises the main issues for pastoral care. So what does the life experience of today's young people make seem obvious or natural?

A recent study has identified significant changes in young people's life experience over the past twenty years. The writers take from their research the contrasting images of journey by train and journey by car.[4]

The train journey acts as a metaphor for youth experience and expectation in the 60s and 70s. At school young people joined one of a number of trains, each

1 Furlong and Cartmel, *Young People and Social Change* (Open University, 1997) p 1.
2 Andrew Walker, *Telling the Story* (SPCK, 1996) p 124.
3 James D Hunter, 'What Is Modernity?' in *Faith and Modernity* Sampson, Samuel and Sugden (eds) (Regnum, 1994) p 13.
4 Furlong and Cartmel, p 6f.

one bound for a different level of personal and social achievement. The point about the train image was that, once on your train, it is difficult to get off. The train pupils boarded was determined primarily by social class, gender and educational achievement. A few may be able to switch destinations but, for most, their place within society follows directly from these factors. Once on a train it is hard to get off, especially as someone else is driving. This image combines a limiting of expectations with an apparent promise of stability—a job or career for life.

The car journey provides a more appropriate metaphor for the life experience and expectations of young people in the eighties and nineties. A long car journey is much more in the hands of the individual who is driving. It involves continual navigational choices. Where you end up depends much more on your own decision making and skill. Practically any destination could be achieved, but making the right choices from primary school on, is critical. And by contrast to the train image, there is no promise of stability or continuity, no job security or career plan for life. In fact an awareness of risk and an awareness of the uncertainty of the future have become part of the mindset of many young people. 'Youth is a period of uncertainty where young people have no clear picture of what the future holds.'[5]

These researchers are quick to point out the fallacies in a view of life which puts everything down to individual choice and ignores continuing social inequalities. But for the moment it will be enough to note that the train image arises in the culture of modernity and the car image in that of postmodernity. This booklet will focus on the pastoral implications of today's young people's experience of postmodern (some prefer late modern) culture.

2
Consumer Culture

The most significant dimension of the shift from modernity to postmodernity is the move from a culture in which personal identity and social integration were found through production and the work-place (and thus making a positive contribution to to a foreseeable better world) to a culture based on consumption, the market and personal choice now. Even sociologists who resist the term 'postmodern' describe the new shape of society as being centred on consumerism. If this is the case with the overall society it is inevitably central to young people's experience of their world. And it will not do simply to bemoan consumerism as though it could be avoided. We might as well invite fish to live out of the water.

'Our culture is within us as well as around us. We cannot escape it, though it is possible to transform, and in other ways alter our use of the culture that we have received.'[6] Consumerism is the social water in which we all swim. The young cannot avoid it. They need to understand it so that they can swim in it and not drown in polluted waters. These sort of social swimming lessons will need to form a major part of the pastoral care offered to them. For the postmodern worldview 'How we consume is an integral part of the kind of person we are, and the kind of person we present to the wider world.'[7] Shopping malls act as the new community centres, the places to hang out, to meet friends and to be seen.

Consumerism has a built-in addictive quality. It maintains itself by combining the promise of pleasure with the built-in obsolescence of whatever it is that is meant to please. 'Young consumers want products and services that are going to do something for them, make them look or feel better, have more fun and be better accepted within their peer group.'[8] The desire for 'the latest' is continually stimulated. Consumer economics only work by the creation of a culture of dissatisfaction rather than contentment.

Consumerism also has a spirituality—or rather an anti-spirituality. A recent sociological study openly claimed that 'Pleasure lies at the heart of consumerism. It finds in consumerism a unique champion which promises to liberate it both from its bondage to sin, duty and morality as well as its ties to faith, spirituality and redemption. Consumerism proclaims pleasure not merely as the right of every individual but also as every individual's obligation to him or her self…The pursuit of pleasure, untarnished by guilt or shame, becomes the new image of the good life.'[9] In practice we shall see that, rather than being essentially hostile to spirituality, consumerism functions as a controlling world-view which reduces spirituality to another consumer item. But there is no doubt that for many a consumer lifestyle is a polite and unquestioned form of hedonism.

Consumer culture also acts as an anaesthetic. It numbs its followers, hiding the poor and disadvantaged, and creating what one financial expert described as 'two-tier world, I'm alright, scenario.' For those who are poor it offers a view of the good life which is economically out of reach. 'Seductive impulses, to be effective, must be transmitted in all directions and addressed indiscriminately to everybody who will listen. But there are more of those who can listen than of those who can respond in the fashion which the seductive message was meant to elicit.'[10] The consumer worldview reduces many people's vision of freedom to freedom to shop. It 'promises something it can't deliver. It actually promises universality of happiness. Everybody is free to choose and if everybody is let into the shop, then everybody is equally happy.'[11] But we do not all have the same access to the shops! And there seems to be a direct connection between consumerism and crime. Every Western consumer society has seen its prison population grow, as some consume

6   Charles Kraft, *Christianity In Culture* (Orbis, 1979) p 106.
7   Wyn and White, *Rethinking Youth* (Sage, 1997) p 86.
8   Gunter and Furnham, *Children As Consumers* (Routledge, 1998) p 170.
9   Yiannis Gabriel and Tim Lang, *The Unmanageable Consumer* (Sage, 1995) p 100.
10 Zygmunt Bauman, *Postmodernity and Its Discontents* (Blackwell, 1997) p 40.
11 Zygmunt Bauman, *Intimations of Postmodernity* (Routledge, 1992) p 225.

illegal substances, steal legal ones, or wreck what they feel excluded from.

The prime value of consumer society is personal choice. 'Choice (is) at the centre of consumerism, both as emblem and core value.'[12] The underlying assumption is that a young person can achieve anything they set their mind to; it is just a matter of choice. 'Today everything is presented as a possibility.'[13] This would be acceptable, even admirable, if it were simply a matter of encouraging young people to set their sights high. But, as we shall see, it becomes a source of anguish and self blame, because it ignores the inequalities of the different starting points and unequal initial resources available to different groups. (We may have moved from trains to cars , but everyone knows that all cars are not equal!)

The consumer mindset has become pervasive. Some years ago the Navigators carried out a survey in Europe, to identify the reasons for their increasing difficulties in leading students to Christ. Their results showed that the students interviewed were not asking if Christianity was 'true,' nor were they asking if Christianity 'worked.' Their key question was, 'Do I like it and would I feel comfortable with it?' In other words, would it make a good consumer choice as I shop for some (not 'a') spirituality? One young lapsed Roman Catholic said that her attraction to Rastafarianism was because 'It's an easy religion to fit into your everyday life. I'm comfortable with it.'

The impact of consumerism on attitudes to truth will be addressed later, but one further dimension of consumer society needs to be identified—the shift of emphasis from the future to the present. 'It is characteristic of our age that there is little sense of community, of any real sense of history, as the present is all that matters.'[14] Individual choice has replaced 'progress' as the core value and belief of our society. Modernity was built on the Enlightenment belief in perpetual human ability to create a better world and the related expectation of an increasingly affluent life. Postmodernity, on the other hand, is marked by uncertainty, irony or plain scepticism about the future, leaving the present as the only thing there is to be sure of. These two stages in Western culture have been illustrated by the contrast between the savings book—making sacrifices now for later benefit, perhaps to the next generation—and the credit card—taking the waiting out of wanting. 'Modernity extolled the delay of gratification;…the postmodern world…preaches delay of payment. If the savings book was the epitome of modern life, the credit card is the paradigm of the postmodern one.'[15]

The loss of belief in progress was demonstrated in the young people who went through their teens in the early eighties to nineties, identified with the music of Kurt Cobain's Nirvana, and were labelled Generation X. This was the first generation expecting to be both better educated and worse off than their parents—which is not how the modern story was meant to work out. Churches are now beginning to minister to these people's children.

12 Gabriel and Lang, p 27.
13 Furlong and Cartmel, p 7.
14 Jon Savage, *Time Travel* (Chatto and Windus, 1996) p 149.
15 Zygmunt Bauman, *Life in Fragments* (Blackwell, 1995) p 5.

3

The Search for Identity

In times of social change people face questions about their personal and corporate identity. In pre-modern times identity was founded on a shared sense of rootedness in the past. In modernity it was found in progress, an ideological hope for the future.

Postmodernity has lost the certainty of its hope for the future and has failed to rediscover any coherent sense of rootedness in the past.

There is of course an awareness of the past, but little sense of the authority of the past. Our histories do not offer guidance about the shape of the future, they merely provide raw materials for making something new. The regular use of the digital sampler, extracting fragments of old pop records as raw materials to make new ones, is both an example and an illustration of this.

Postmodernity has neither the pre-modern world's belief in the authority of the past nor the modern world's ideological confidence in the future. But a stable sense of personal identity requires 'the capacity to keep a particular narrative going. The individual's biography...must continually integrate events which occur in the external world, and sort them into the ongoing "story" about the self.'[16] At the heart of a sense of identity is a story we tell ourselves about ourselves and which carries a measure of conviction. But the postmodern world can only offer 'A self with no given continuities, save those of the body which is its bearer and of the memory which to the best of its ability gathers in its past.'[17]

Postmodern theory challenges the credibility of 'grand narratives'—stories or beliefs which provide the key to the overall meaning of life. But if our society no longer believes in the 'grand narrative' of progress and has replaced it with little narratives of individual consumer choice then each of us is alone—we have no common story to share, beyond the consumer one. 'Men and women have been left alone with their fears; they are told by philosophers that the void is here to stay, and by politicians that coping with it is their own duty and worry...The social world appears to the individual as a pool of choices, a market to be exact.'[18] The transition from a production or workplace focused culture to a consumer one is also reflected in changes to the assumed understanding of identity. 'While the locus of modern identity revolved around one's occupation, one's function in the public sphere (or family), postmodern identity revolves around leisure, centred on looks, images and consumption. Modern identity was a serious affair involving fundamental choices that defined who one was (profession, family, etc), while postmodern identity is a function of leisure and is grounded in play, in games-

16 Anthony Giddens, *Modernity and Self-Identity* (Polity, 1991) p 54.
17 Alasdair MacIntyre, *After Virtue* (Duckworth, 1985) p 33.
18 Zygmunt Bauman, *Intimations*, p xviii.

manship.'[19] As we shall see these are very serious games, however playfully or ironically they are played.

Today's teenagers have been born into a world in which it is 'normal' to construct your identity, to make yourself who you want to be, through consumer choice. 'Consumption and lifestyles have become central to the process of identity construction.'[20] Identity is a prime pastoral issue for it is closely related to self-worth. 'To have is to be. For many western young people at the end of the twentieth century the belief "I am what I consume and what I have" remains strong…Possessions in the form of consumer goods…are related to both self-esteem and well-being.'[21] Studies of magazines marketed for teenage girls (and read by thousands of twelve year olds) have shown, for example, that they simultaneously build their readers sense of being intelligent and discriminating, while inducting them as young consumers. Intelligence is about exercising your new freedom to consume, not about questioning the consumer approach to identity.

Underlying this consumer approach to identity is a deeper assumption—that identity is a matter of personal construction in the first place. If there are no authoritative givens from the past or grand dreams of the future you simply make yourself up. 'If identities are essentially forms of social construction, then one can be anything at any time.'[22]

This is of course a fantasy. However individualistic a world view we may have, we all live under substantial constraints. When Michael Jackson performed at the Brit awards a few years ago he caused a major stir by acting out a Jesus-like role, apparently without any sense of irony. If you are Michael Jackson and have almost unlimited resources you can convince yourself that you can be anyone or anything you want; but all the performance did was to demonstrate how far from reality Jackson was.

Just as consumerism promises happiness but creates a culture of disappointment, so contemporary culture promises freedom, but creates instability. The lyric of a highly successful dance hit went 'You're free to do what you want to do, you've gotta live your life, do what you want to.' But we are not as free as the song supposes. There are limitations built into the way we were made, the purpose for which we were made and in the social and political contexts into which we were born. This illusion of unlimited freedom is a misinterpretation of our society's loss of any sense of stable core or givenness in human identity. 'In place of an enduring core of deep and indelible character, there is a chorus of invitations. Each invitation "to be" also casts doubt on the wisdom and authenticity of the others.'[23]

The sense of inability to find a core of identity, or to break free, was beautifully

---

19 Douglas Kellner, 'Constructing Postmodern Identities' in *Modernity and Identity*, Lash and Friedman (eds) (Blackwell, 1992) p 153.
20 Furlong and Cartmel, p 9.
21 Gunter and Furnham, p 43.
22 Kenneth Gergen, *The Saturated Self* (Basic Books, 1991) p 184.
23 Kenneth Gergen, p 174.

expressed in The Verve's song *Bitter Sweet Symphony*. 'No change, I can't change, But I'm here in my mould, I am here in my mould. But I'm a million different people from one day to the next, I can't change my mould.' Left to itself the consumer culture which is targeted at young people can only create a highly unstable sense of identity. 'The overwhelming variety of...possibilities for identity, in an affluent image culture no doubt create highly unstable identities while constantly providing new openings to restructure one's identity.'[24]

Some young people thrive on the freedom this offers, helping to develop an adult culture which, as we shall see, has many adolescent characteristics. But others find it hard to cope. Just a the Hindu seek release from the constant cycle of rebirth, so some young people long to escape the treadmill of continually making yourself up. Psychologically some shrink to 'minimal selves.' 'The self 'contracts to a defensive core.'[25] They search for a fixed point around which to build their lives. The young person whose available hours are totally absorbed by computer games could be one example. Some drug use provides another. In the film *Train Spotting* one heroin addict describes his addiction as providing 'the one thing' that gives his life focus.

Generally speaking, those young people who have had a stable upbringing and inherited some sense of values from their parents survive better than those who feel alone on the sea of choice. When deeply unstable characters like Kurt Cobain are widely accepted as role models something is clearly wrong. At the heart of all this is a crisis of self worth. It is not a coincidence that the French philosopher who has encapsulated the loss of belief in 'grand narratives' also wrote, 'Each of us knows that our self does not amount to much.'[26]

4

Temporary Communities

'Consumer society is individualistic by definition,'[27] but humans are social animals. Paradoxically a consumer society, with all its emphasis on individual choice, is one where what others think of us becomes increasingly important. One American sociologist has shown that the move from the pre-modern era, through the modern and on to the postmodern has been a move from 'tradition-directed types,' that is people who find their identity in the structures and traditions handed down to them, to 'inner-directed types,' that is people for whom personal conscience

24 Douglas Kellner, p 174.
25 Christopher Lasch, *The Minimal Self*, p 1.
26 Jean-Francois Lyotard, *The Postmodern Condition* (Manchester, 1984).
27 Petta Sulkenen, *Constructing the New Consumer Society* (Macmillan, 1997) p 6.

and inner conviction is at the core of identity; and now to 'other-directed types' that is people for whom approval from others is 'their chief source of direction and chief area of sensitivity.'[28] Paradoxically, in a culture which claims to believe that we can be whatever we want to be, what our peers think of us is a dominant factor in the establishing of identity.

This is a culture of temporary allegiances and communities, of many encounters but few relationships. If identity is a matter of consumer choice, then it can vary depending on whom you choose to hang around with. Some writers have described the shifting commitments of people relating to one another on the basis of brands, styles and trends in music as 'tribal.' 'Tribal groupings cohere on the basis of their own minor values, and...attract and collide with each other in an endless dance.'[29] 'Image and style are now central to identity. Nike running shoes, Levi jeans, Coca-Cola, these and more, all help to give shape to who we are...Likewise our social circle, our peer group, is likely to share consuming patterns in common, more than anything else.'[30] Interestingly, this pattern of finding identity through temporary tribes is recognized as being nomadic. Western consumers are nomads, they have 'no abiding city,' but continually move on from temporary allegiance to temporary allegiance.[31] Some of these shifting communities are gathered around events—a festival, a protest march, a match or a club night. What matters most is being seen—'Been (seen) there, done that!' There is an illusion of community, and there can be genuinely committed friendships but the overall ethos is one of 'imagined communities...I am seen therefore I exist.'[32]

It needs to be emphasized that I am not describing something peculiar to youth culture. Rather this is the emerging pattern of the overall Western culture, including the world of young people. The 'generation gap,' as the term has been used over the past 30-40 years no longer exists in its original form. It has been replaced by 'a bewildering range of subcultural groupings sending out messages of identity to anyone who will hear...The custom designed life-style is no longer the province of youth. In the words of style critic Robert Elms, nobody is a "teenager" any more, because everybody is.'[33] This is illustrated by the marketing term 'middle youth,' which refers to the ability of bands like The Verve and Radiohead to appeal both to teenagers and students and to middle-aged fans like myself. Significantly, most of the 'middle youth' acts are raising questions about identity.

The youth service in the UK no longer defines itself by a specific age group and definitions of youth are 'coming to be distinguished not by generational age, but by a particular set of lifestyle choices and consumption practices—taste rather than age coming to be the defining feature of "youth" culture.'[34]

28 David Riesman in *Postemotional Society*, Stjepan Mestrovic (Sage, 1997) p 91.
29 Michel Maffelosi, quoted in Rojek, *Decentring Leisure* (Sage, 1995) p 151.
30 David Lyon, 'Memory and the Millennium' in *Grace and Truth in the Secular Age*, Bradshaw (ed) (1998) p 284.
31 Chris Rojek, *Decentering Leisure* pp 151-2.
32 Zygmunt Bauman, *Intimations*, p xviiif.
33 *Fashion and Style*, Mike Starkey (Monarch, 1995) p 76.
34 Bill Osgerby, *Youth In Britain Since 1945* (Blackwell, 1998) p 207.

5
Transitions

The transition from youth to adulthood has usually involved three transitions; from school to work; from singleness to marriage or cohabitation; and from the parental home to a place of one's own. Over the last twenty years all of these transitions have changed. A combination of the increase in the number going on to higher education, and the drastic decline in youth employment, has extended the period when young people are at least semi-dependent on their parents. Nutritional developments have resulted in an earlier onset of puberty. Young people are now sexually experienced earlier but, on average, marry later. For various reasons, the average age for leaving home is now younger. The overall effect of these changes is to weaken family ties. The cultural assumptions shared both by young people and their parents value independence at the very same time as the young person's period of economic semi-dependence has been extended. 'The desire to establish the basis for independent lifestyles has become particularly significant.'[35]

As society has changed, so the traditional links between family, school and work have been weakened. The sense of risk in making choices about work, home and sexual partners is one of the primary factors contributing to the sense that 'Young people today are growing up in a different world to that experienced by previous generations,' because they are 'subject to uncertainties which were not part of day to day life for previous generations.'[36] The effect of this is 'an increasing isolation from adult worlds.'[37] As a consequence the peer group, which has always had a critical role for adolescents, has increased in influence. But youth culture, the social context of peer groups, is not stable. Because it shares the shifting alliances and fashion changes of the larger consumer culture it is itself fragmented. Parents nurtured in the sixties era of counter culture, or the seventies punk rebellion, need to be careful they do not read the same sense of a shared movement into the nineties. It is not there.

When an event unites a large section of youth and young adult culture it is the exception that proves the rule. The most significant example was the suicide of Kurt Cobain, the leader of the rock group Nirvana. The response to his death involved a temporary unification of a fragmented youth culture; just as, later, the response to the death of Princess Diana was to have the same effect on the overall culture. Paradoxically both of these deaths revealed, by contrast, the lack of any coherence in our everyday societies, beyond that provided by consumerism. Damon Albarn, lead singer of Blur, wrote how the death of Cobain 'showed me

---

35 Furlong and Cartmel, p 52.
36 Furlong and Cartmel, p 5.
37 Furlong and Cartmel, p 9.

how fragmented the world is the rest of the time, and if there's a key to the Nineties I think it's that perpetual insecurity. Never have people thought so hard about their lives and come to such indecision, or felt further apart. We're powerless and confused—by politics and work and sex and even things like morality.'[38]

6

Who Knows?

The chief characteristic of the postmodern age is uncertainty. Not just uncertainty about the future, but uncertainty about belief.

The chief intellectual enemy of the gospel in modernity was secularism. In postmodernity that role is fulfilled by relativism. Young people are reared in an information age. They are bombarded with information and with competing claims to truth about almost everything. There is no overarching worldview. 'Radio, television and newspapers became elements in a general explosion and proliferation of worldviews.'[39]

The mass media work competitively. Each programme, paper or magazine competes for their version of the truth. They also work sceptically; every claim made in an interview can expect to be challenged or contrasted with an alternative opinion. This creates a culture in which there are so many claims to truth that no one view can plausibly claim to be 'the truth' about anything, and in which all truth claims are greeted with suspicion. In postmodern culture all truths are relative except the truth that all truths are relative.

If the young grow up in a world of competing truth claims, none of which seems to be able to claim authority or authenticity over against the others, they will inevitably drop back on their societies' foundational beliefs as the means by which they discriminate. In other words they will treat truth claims as consumer choices. 'When many voices can be heard, who can say that one should be heeded more than another?...When the only criteria left for choosing between them are learned in the marketplace, then truth appears as a commodity. We hear the people "buy into" a belief or that, rather than rejecting a dogma as false, they "cannot buy" this or that viewpoint.'[40] Matters of belief can then be settled by a pick-and-mix approach, creating a continually changing concoction of the beliefs we like.

This is also very postmodern. All commitments must be provisional, if not temporary, because they are rooted in irony, rather than conviction. A society of

---

38 Damon Albarn in *The Face*.
39 Gianni Vattimo, *The Transparent Society* (Polity, 1992) p 5.
40 David Lyon, *Memory and the Millennium*, p 285.

this sort shapes people who 'have lost the capacity for faith. There are too many alternatives, choices, and interpretations, all of which can be debunked or deconstructed to allow faith in his or her decisions to act.'[41] U2 summed it up well in their song about consumer culture *Zooropa* 'And I have no compass, and I have no map, and I have no reason, no reason to get back. And I have no religion, and I don't know what's what, and I don't know the limit, the limit of what we got.'[42]

The experience of living in a supermarket of truth claims also gives plausibility to another postmodern idea: that anyone trying to convince someone else of a truth or moral value is in fact on a power trip. In some recent thought all talk of truth is reduced to talk of power. So a rather insecure and nervous Christian Union group in a school or college can be accused of 'trying to ram their truth down our throat' just for making the attempt to share their faith, irrespective of how they did it.

The immediate pastoral implications of this require a particular sensitivity to any appearance of manipulating young people for our own ideological or personal ends, combined with the determination to continue to take the risk of love and commitment to young people.

7

Spirituality—Yes; Church—No

The postmodern age combines a spiritual hunger with a profound distrust of authoritative institutions, including religious ones. Spirituality is back in the public square, but any and every spirituality, and there are no maps. The hunger is real. Chris Carter, the creator of the X Files wrote, 'I'm a non-religious person looking for a religious experience.' He made his main character Mulder in his own image in this respect. Patsy Palmer, the actress who plays Bianca in East Enders, said in an interview 'I've really got into reading books on spirituality. I feel that I've got a hole inside me, you know? You try and fill it up with all these things but there's nothing that can make you happy.' Many other celebrities, whom young people treat as role models, have made similar statements.

But Patsy Palmer, and many like her, are not reading the Bible, they are reading the *Celestine Prophecy* and similar books. People, young and old, in the West are searching for spiritual answers, but the last place they expect to find them is in the Christian church. The institutional church is assumed to be part of the old ('modern'!) order that has failed. We live at a transition time in our history when

---

41 Mestrovic, p 118.
42 U2, *Zooropa*, Island Records CD, 1993.

all ancient institutions are being questioned. 'The closing decades of the twentieth century [are] a critical moment in the religious history of this country...decades
in which both traditional institutions and traditional certainties struggle, in secular as well as religious life...but a society in which "spiritual stirrings"—of a widely
diverse, not necessarily conventional and frequently contradictory nature—are
widespread.'[43] Some of this is a quest for spiritual experiences rather than for
God. A consumer society encourages a quest for a religious buzz, rather than for
a life of discipleship. 'The contemporary climate is therapeutic not religious. People hunger not for personal salvation...but for the feeling, the momentary illusion, of personal well-being.'[44]

Christian pastoral work with young people will need to re-establish the link
between spirituality and ethics. As David Wells has written, 'the New Testament
never promises anyone a life of psychological wholeness or offers a guarantee of
the consumer's satisfaction with Christ...As beings made in God's image we are
fundamentally moral beings, not consumers. The satisfaction of our psychological needs pales in significance when compared with the enduring value of doing
what is right.'[45]

The most creative and culturally significant development in youth and young
adult culture since the mid-eighties has been the extraordinary growth of the
dance and club culture. It has combined all the strengths, weaknesses, aspirations
and contradictions of postmodern culture. There has been an extraordinary crea-
tivity in music and electronic imagery. There has been a commercial manipula-
tion. There has been the widespread use of the drug ecstasy (much of the music is
created so that, at club volumes, it is 'best' experienced during an ecstasy trip).
There has been unrestrained hedonism (including some of the most sexually ex-
plicit music yet seen in the charts—'I've seen you around, I find you very attractive, will you go to bed with me?').

There has also been a sense of community. A club is a 'temporary community.'
The contacts made there are not likely to spill over into the rest of life. The problem with a night spent clubbing is its lack of connection to a normal Monday to
Friday. But the combination of a shared enthusiasm for the dance scene and ecstasy's effect of lowering the emotional boundaries between people has created a
real sense of community and, in some, a longing for a more stable expression of it.

'Rave is more than music and drugs; it's a matrix of lifestyle, ritualized behav-
iour and beliefs. To the participant it feels like a religion.'[46] A band called Faithless
(!) beautifully described the sense of sanctuary many find in the club scene. 'This
is my church. This is where I heal my hurt. For tonight God is a DJ.'[47] To some
artists and participants (usually more middle class) dance culture has also been a
vehicle to spiritual enlightenment, to an experience of the transcendent, not just

43 Grace Davie, *Religion in Britain Since 1945* (Blackwell, 1994) p 190.
44 Christopher Lasch, *The Culture of Narcissism*.
45 David Wells, *God in the Wasteland* (IVP, 1994) p 115.
46 Simon Reynolds, *Energy Flash* (Picador, 1998) p xviii.
47 Faithless, 'God is a DJ' from the Cheeky records CD, *Sunday 8PM*.

of a chemically stimulated community. The boundary between finding God for God's sake, and seeking a spiritual as well as a chemical high, is wafer thin at this point, and some of the most thoughtful supporters of the dance scene have raised questions. 'I worry sometimes whether recreational drug use is any kind of adequate basis for a culture, let alone a counterculture. Is rave simply about the dissipation of utopian energies into the void, or does the idealism it catalyses spill over into and transform ordinary life?...Learning to 'lose your self' can be an enlightenment, but it can also be strangely selfish: a greed for intense, ravishing experiences.'[48] But, at very least, a spiritual quest is present in the dance scene.

Another reason for this spiritual quest is that our society has lost its sense of overall purpose. 'Western civilisation suffers from a strong sense of moral and spiritual exhaustion. Having constructed a society of unprecedented sophistication, convenience and prosperity, nobody can remember what it was supposed to be for.'[49] Purpose is a spiritual issue and, as Lesslie Newbigin loved to point out 'The human spirit cannot live permanently with the form of rationality which has no answer to the question "why?"'[50]

We are at a critical moment for the church. Many of the young are perfectly content with the comforts of consumerism. They know no other world. Some are very idealistic and will pour their energy into specific issues of concern, such as the environment and human rights. An increasing number have an openness to some form of spirituality. But in the European Values Survey of 1989 people were asked to list 13 institutions in order of confidence. Those over 50 rated church third out of thirteen. Those under 35 ranked it bottom. That is to say they regarded the church as totally irrelevant. Sunday attendance at Anglican churches by 14-17 year olds has dropped by 34.9% since 1987 and that of 18-21 year olds by 34.1%. Church-based youth work that does not require church attendance has declined by similar figures.[51]

The Price of Uncertainty

And rarely have young people needed the church more. In practice young people are growing up in a world characterized by risk while being told that everything depends on their individual choices. 'Overall, young people's futures have begun to look much less secure. By the mid-nineties the pace of technological change and greater economic instability had made it more difficult to predict young people's occupational biographies with any certainty...Even youngsters in possession of skills and qualifications felt less confident about their future...With traditional certainties disrupted and undermined, youngsters' life choices seemed to carry a much greater degree of risk.'[52]

Many young people pay the price of this uncertainty in their own bodies and

48 Simon Reynolds, *Energy Flash* (Picador, 1998) p xix.
49 Clifford Longley's forward to *Faith in the Future*, Jonathan Sacks (DLT, 1995).
50 Lesslie Newbigin, *The Gospel in a Pluralist Society* (SPCK, 1989) p 213
51 *Youth A Part* (Church House Press, 1996) p 13.
52 Bill Osgerby, p 205f.

personalities. 'Depression, eating disorders, suicide and attempted suicide have all become more common and can be seen as reflecting...the ongoing sense of doubt which is a central feature of high modernity and which can be particularly threatening for young people in the process of establishing adult identities.'[53] The percentage increases for these conditions are not large (with the marked exception of teenagers who say they have at some time considered suicide!). But the direction of change is quite clear. This writer was particularly shocked to discover that teenage suicide is a growing factor in South African townships, since the consumer dream replaced the Struggle as the aspiration of young men.

The question of celebrity role models has already been mentioned. One journalist reflecting on the public response to the death of Diana wrote 'The young seek role models not among the contented but among those before whom the world has dangled every pleasure and yet snatched it away: the much-married actress, the self-abusing rock star, the Duchess of York and the queen of them all, Diana, Princess of Wales. People seem to take comfort in watching the famous find life as hard as they do themselves. Diana was news when happy. She was bigger news when unhappy.'[54]

The increase in marriage breakdown also contributes to anxiety and instability. Since the 1960s there has been a four-fold increase in divorce. Between 1971 and 1989 the number of children in lone parent families increased by 300%. One researcher has argued that 'by the age of 16, around one in four young people will have experienced the divorce of their parents and many of these will spend time living in a reconstituted family.'[55] In postmodern society there is a greater awareness of the uncertainty of the future. On the whole we no longer believe in a straightforward human control of history. Professor Anthony Giddens (who dislikes the term postmodern) makes the contrast in this way. 'Living in the modern world is more like being aboard a careering juggernaut rather than being in a carefully controlled and well-driven motor car.'[56] In this illustration the car, carefully controlled (and probably built) by the driver was completing a carefully planned journey to an inevitably better world (progress). Instead human life and development is portrayed as trying to control a runaway lorry. Risk and uncertainty are the realities of everyday experience.

Giddens and other writers recognize that this results in high levels of anxiety and the erosion of trust in the safety of the world. He points out the paradox that many people cope with this anxiety by believing in fate. 'Fate, a feeling that things will take their own course anyway, thus reappears at the core of a world which is supposedly taking rational control of its own affairs.'[57] If the bullet of postmodern life has your number on it there is nothing you can do! This, as much as an openness to spirituality, explains the influence of astrology in technological societies.

53 Furlong and Cartmel, p 80f.
54 *The Times*
55 Haskey quoted in Furlong and Cartmel, p 47.
56 Anthony Giddens, *The Consequences of Modernity* (Polity, 1990) p 53.
57 Giddens, *Consequences*, p 133f.

8
Summary—Fallen Contradictions

I have attempted to outline the contemporary context in which young people live their lives and the social forces which affect them. I have relied mainly on the findings of sociological research. I have described the water in which young people will either swim or drown. Some writers describe this as a necessarily nomadic existence. The journey may now be by car, but there are no maps and no self-evident destination. 'We all become nomads, migrating across a system that is too vast to be our own, but in which we are fully involved, translating and transforming bits and elements into local instances of sense.'[58]

Many of them are determined both to cope with all the risks and to maintain their personal authenticity. They need all the help the church can give them.

One of the many paradoxes of the postmodern world is that there is a great emphasis on image, appearance and style. 'Enjoy the surface' is a piece of postmodern wisdom. Style-based magazines flourished in the mid-eighties and nineties. Yet when the original style magazine, *The Face*, gave a whole issue to a review of the nineties it was the problem of identity which dominated its analysis. The magazine which celebrated the surface had no choice but to look beneath the surface and ask if anything was there.

In the lead article an associate editor wrote, 'The Nineties quest for life and some sort of authenticity, coupled with a gradual loss of faith in the capacity of big ideals to save our souls, has led us to make up our own truths, build our own small worlds as best we can. These days, people try to create their own disparate, genuine societies within the larger uniform fake one on offer, and they're doing it in innumerable, almost unquantifiable ways.'[59]

This short paragraph sums up most of the themes I have covered: the loss of faith in big ideals (grand stories), truth that is constructed rather than discovered, the awareness of the shallowness (fake) of consumerism, the urgent need for community and for imagination to cope with a world that has changed.

If some people find the uncertainty of postmodernity daunting, others believe it is a price well worth paying for a new freedom. 'Don't get tied down' could well be the catch phrase of postmodernity. 'An ever growing number of postmodern men and women...find the open-endedness of their situation attractive enough to outweigh the anguish of uncertainty.'[60] Like much of the material above this is a characteristic of the overall culture which is also a feature of youth culture. 'Instead of making a firm set of stylistic commitments most youngsters have

---

58 Iain Chambers 'Cities Without Maps' in *Mapping the Futures*, Bird (ed) (Routledge, 1993) p 193.
59 Miranda Sawyer in *The Face*.
60 Zygmunt Bauman, *Discontents*, p 13.

instead cruised across a range of affiliations, constantly forming and reforming their identities according to social context.'[61]

Another paradox of postmodernity is that the search for, or construction of, identity that is perhaps its greatest concern, turns out to have a hidden agenda; the avoidance of being answerable to anyone apart from myself. 'The hub of postmodern life-strategy is not identity building but avoidance of fixation.' 'Keep the options open.'[62]

The American philosopher Richard Rorty has argued that our identity is entirely a human social construction and that 'there is no centre to the self.'[63] He then says there are simply 'different ways of weaving' new ideas and beliefs into our personal histories. In other words, with some political or economic limits, you can be whatever you want to be, and all options are equal. A reply has come from Miroslav Volf of Fuller Seminary. Volf refers to Galatians 2.19-20 and denies that the human self, created by God, is without a given centre. 'Paul' he says 'presumes a centred self, more precisely a wrongly centred self that needs to be decentred by being nailed to the cross: "I have been crucified with Christ" (Gal 2.19-20). Though the self may lack an "objective" and "immovable" centre, the self is never without a centre; it is always engaging in the production of its own centre.' Volf goes on to emphasize the self-centredness with which fallen humans make many of their choices, and do so at the cost of others. In this light Rorty's use of the word 'weaving' for the creation of postmodern identity is naive. '"Weaving" (Rorty) would be a rather innocent way to describe this production... "Struggle" and "Violence" come closer to being an adequate description.'[64]

The postmodern self tries to construct its own continuously changing centre, just as the modern self claimed that it was the centre of everything. 'Whichever way the centring takes place and whatever its result, the self should be de-centred, claims Paul...then a recentering of that same self can take place...The centre is Jesus Christ crucified and resurrected who has become part and parcel of the very structure of the self...At the centre of the (new) self lies self giving love.'[65] How then may believers in Jesus Christ apply the challenge of the cross and exercise a pastoral ministry to postmodern young people?

61 Bill Osgerby, p 203.
62 Zygmunt Bauman, *Discontents*, p 13.
63 Richard Rorty, *Contingency, Irony and Solidarity* (Cambridge, 1989) p 83f
64 Miroslav Volf, *Exclusion and Embrace* (Abingdon, 1996) p 69. ·
65 Volf, p 70f.

9
Pastoral Responses

An immediate response may be that this booklet should have been in the evangelism series rather than the pastoral one. However 'In the new cultural landscape pastoral care is perhaps the most important means of mission.'[66] The care of young people is an essential prerequisite to winning them for Christ. The advice I will offer will often be as appropriate for not-yet-Christians as for Christian young people.

Protect and Survive?

The immediate response of many pastors and parents, and as a result, the pressure and expectations put on many youth leaders, will be to major on pastoral care through protection. The culture I have outlined will be seen as offering far more danger than it gives opportunity to Christian adolescents. Protection is a well established strategy. Pete Ward has argued persuasively that 'safety' is the underlying function of much Evangelical youth work. 'Parents are concerned that their children should be protected and kept safe from what they regard as the disturbing and dangerous world which threatens to engulf them during their adolescence. In this context youth work becomes the means by which Christian parents seek to extend their influence on teenagers who are seeking more independence and freedom from home.'[67]

The Christian subculture of record companies, theatre groups and annual events then provides the safe alternative environment. This carries over into the culture of some college Christian Unions with their tradition of making sure that the main midweek meeting occurs on the same night as the main social events in the Students Union.

There are a number of flaws, theological and pastoral, with this strategy. It involves a serious misreading of the significance of the world in God's purposes. A fallen culture is a dangerous place, but it is also the object of God's love through Christ. The God who sends his rain on the just and the unjust has never withdrawn his hand from his creation. He is still committed to the world. 'God's commitment is a continuing personal activity that supports the created order.'[68] Humans are made in his image to partner him in this activity. 'Because of God's presence and action, our involvement in culture has real theological significance. We are called to reflect God's own commitment to the world.'[69] God's hands are already upon everything that our hands touch. His mind already sustains everything that our minds address. The world is not a place from which he is absent,

66 Paul Goodliff, *Care In A Confused Climate* (DLT, 1998) p 11.
67 Pete Ward, *Growing Up Evangelical* (SPCK, 1996) p 166.
68 William Dyrness, *The Earth is God's* (Orbis, 1997) p 36.
69 William Dyrness, p 69.

however much it may grieve him. The work of God in Christ brings redemption into this creation-sustaining activity. 'In Christ God becomes a part of creation, God is embodied.'[70] 'If the incarnation shows us anything, it is that God comes to us and is known by us in and through the created order. This makes our embodied obedience—our face-to-face encounters with others, the practice of our work, and our stewardship of the goods of creation—either vehicles of praise or expressions of our indifference to God.'[71] If these insights by an Evangelical scholar are right then a culture of protection of our young may inadvertently reflect an indifference to God's purposes in Christ for the earth. 'We do God's will...by working alongside God in bringing people and the earth to the place where they reflect the divine glory.'[72] The 'safety' model also displays a serious misreading of the power of 'the world' in its negative biblical sense. The nature of pervasive cultural values is such that it is no protection to provide an alternative world. It really is possible to be 'of the world but not in it.' The interlock between the world, the flesh and the Devil ensures that there is no Christian environment that automatically guarantees safety. Furthermore many Christian parents are highly selective when it comes to the features of 'the world' that necessitate protection. They will rightly want their children protected from promiscuous sex and the dangers of drug abuse, but many are more comfortable with consumerism than, this book suggests, might be good for their spiritual health.

A further flaw with the safety strategy is that it too easily sets pastoral care against evangelism. 'The problem with the church-based youth fellowship is that "unchurched" young people can easily be seen as a significant threat.'[73] The very young people who are most in need of the gospel become the undesirables who might infect the existing members. It can, in fact, work the other way, with council estate converts pressing their parents for the expensive trainers which mark out the in-group of a more middle class youth group.

Another flaw in the safety strategy is rooted in a failure to grasp the extent of the changes in youth experience which I have described. We all tend to believe that our children are going through what we went through, if we were believers when in our teens. So all we have to do is to pass on our experience, or expect the youth leader to do it for us. But, 'The world that our parents knew is not the world we live in today; nor is our world any sure guide to the way our children will live and love and work.'[74] I have had to recognize that I do not fully understand the world in which my teenage daughters are called to be faithful to Christ. My studies, along with my conversations with them, have shown me how different it is from the world of my teenage experience. Some (but not all) of my experience is about as useful to them as King Saul's armour was to young David for the battle with Goliath. I have learnt that Christian parenthood is a matter of trust.

70 William Dyrness, p 15.
71 William Dyrness, p xiv.
72 William Dyrness, p 58.
73 Pete Ward, p 185.
74 Charles Handy, *The Age of Unreason* (Arrow, 1995) p 203.

First I must trust that the world in which my daughters live is not alien to God. 'We share a world where Christ continues to rule through the Holy Spirit so that culture as well as creation is upheld by his presence.'[75] I sometimes think we Christian parents really believe that 'he who is in the world is greater than he who is in our children.'

God's equipment for his church involves a vital partnership of Word and Spirit. This partnership is of extra importance in a time of cultural transition. The Word (in the sense of the Scriptures—the word about the Word) is God's living message, his gift from the past. It is the authoritative and supreme record of who our God is, what he has done, and how his people are to live. It is critical that we arm our young people with an understanding of Scripture. 'Scripture is a means of grace by which God's Word continues to come to us. It is not so much a static collection of timeless oracles as it is the place to stand when one wants to be in God's presence and learn of him.'[76]

The Spirit is the gift of God from the future. The Spirit is the foretaste and guarantee of the future Christ has won. 'The action of the Spirit is to anticipate, in the present and by means of the finite and contingent, the things of the age to come.'[77] Parents and youth leaders alike have to trust the Spirit who comes from the future. His calling is to enable each generation to live faithfully as a foretaste of God's coming kingdom. He did it for our own generation, we can trust him to do it for our children, however different their world may be.

The remaining fallacy with the safety model is that it assumes a misunderstanding of holiness. At the heart of the biblical understanding of holiness is the idea of being separate so as to be distinctive. This was a vital strategy when Old Testament Israel consisted of one nation in the promised land. But when Christ comes; 'when God moves towards humanity and takes up residence, then the emphasis shifts from separation to involvement.'[78] Involvement is essential because the gospel has now to be lived out and proclaimed in all cultures. Distinctiveness is also essential, or we have nothing to proclaim.

How then do we care for young people in such a way that they are equipped by God to live in a Christlike way in the everyday world of their peers?

Model the Practice of Discernment

I have not intended to suggest that young people have no need of some form of youth group. The question is what is the group for? There is a critical difference between a counter-culture and a sub-culture. A sub-culture reflects the main values of a cultural era and applies them to a particular group within it. The group need have little contact with other subcultures; it is shaped by the overarching culture. The chief aim of this book has been to outline the contemporary features of this shaping. A counter-culture offers a different view of the overarching story

75 William Dyrness, p 83.
76 Clark Pinnock, *The Scripture Principle* (Hodder, 1985) p 163f.
77 Colin Gunton, *The Promise of Trinitarian Theology* (T and T Clark, 1991) p 68.
78 Mike Riddell, *Threshold of the Future* (SPCK, 1998) p 73.

and may offer an alternative pattern of overall belief. This is a primary purpose of the church's work with young people.

We saw earlier that beliefs are given plausibility by the way they seem to work out in culture. Many young people regard the values and beliefs of postmodernity as 'obvious' because they have never experienced an alternative plausibility. A counter-cultural youth work will aim chiefly at showing young Christians and not-yet-Christians how to live for Christ in the world. It will try to model a scripturally-based discernment guided by the Holy Spirit. This will almost certainly involve (youth workers not parents) accompanying young people to clubs, movies and concerts—not as escorts but as companions (and sometimes as pupils—ask them to show you their world). Young people need help in learning the principled handling of choice. The focus of the work will be as much in the young person's world of school and leisure as in the youth meeting or church group night out. Be with them and help them to discover how to live the gospel where they are.

An Alternative Plausibility—Christian Community

As long as the group finds its focus in Christian discipleship in the real world, its meetings and relationships can be of great importance. A relationship with a youth leader and with Christian friends may be the first taste of trustworthy relationships that some young people have ever had. They will often be both suspicious of them and attracted to them. God made them to grow through stable loving relationships. Ongoing commitment and an apparent inability to be shocked need combining with the willingness to confront and speak the truth when it needs speaking. Correction or challenge without rejection is a new experience for many. Only in this way will young people move beyond the superficialities of image and learn to make commitments.

The major postmodern issue is that of identity. In the context of Christian community and discipleship young people can learn that they are creatures before they are creators—that they are not free to make anything they like of their life and their world, because they were made for a purpose. To know who we are, we need to be willing to be answerable to the one who made us. This is the challenge of the cross, as much a stumbling block in the twentieth and twenty-first centuries as it was in the first. We are constructors of culture, but we are constructors under licence, called to construct a world which reflects and honours its Maker.

In all of this the role of the assurance of salvation is central. Postmodernity is marked by uncertainty and is reacting against modernity's overemphasis on certainty. When the Enlightenment thinking about rational certainty emerged it was countered by Edwards, Whitfield and Wesley not with an equivalent religious certainty (for it is not possible to prove that God loves you with the theological equivalent of a microscope) but with the meeting of Word and Spirit in the doctrine of assurance.[79] The objectivity of the scriptural gospel and the personal witness of

---

79 See David Bebbington, *Evangelicalism in Modern Britain* (Routledge, 1993) pp 42-50.

the Spirit in the new believer combined to give evidence that an individual was indeed Christ's.

In the Evangelical Revival this took place in a culture which had a new confidence in human experience and which had started to believe you could be sure about many things. We have now entered a culture where we are unsure about almost everything. When young people take the risk of trusting in Christ and are part of a community that follows him, they begin to see that this is no longer a matter of how they feel at the moment, but that they are among peers who follow the same Lord and who are putting the same Scriptures to the test. This time assurance dare not be an individualist's charter, but it will prove equally important. Because of the importance of the Christian community in this strategy, and because the community I am arguing for is active in the everyday culture, it is likely that many young people of no Christian background will start to belong to the community before they are sure they can trust the message about its Saviour and Lord.

A Future Worth Living For

The power of consumerism lies in its promise of satisfaction in the present, when the future seems uncertain. The pastoral counter to consumerism must then be based in the hope of a future that is worth living for. Once again the ministry of the Holy Spirit provides the key. In the New Testament the Spirit is 'The certain evidence that the future had dawned, and the absolute guarantee of its final consummation.'[80] This culture seeks experiences for their own sake. Within a Christian community which is actively seeking the world's good, because of the future it believes in, young people learn to understand their experience of the Spirit as a promise about the future as well as a confirmation of what they have believed in the present. This must, of course, be accompanied by scriptural teaching that interprets the work of the Spirit in this way.

Once a vision of God's future and of our involvement in it is established, it creates a alternative image of the 'good life' to that of consumerism. It can strengthen a young person's will to make appropriate sacrifices in the present for the sake of God's calling, to a personal and positive vocation, as a witness to that future today. Because consumerism hides the poor it should be a norm that youth ministry involves an active ministry to the poor. All this puts shopping back in its place and offers something far better. The gospel quality of contentment is rooted in a combination of assurance and God's calling to bear witness to his future world.

It may be necessary to pray and support a young person through the breaking of some addictive habits. Addiction is part of the motor of a consumer society. Some young people should stay away from old haunts and acquaintances until the power of an addictive process is weakened.

There is much more that could be said about the pastoral care of postmodern

---

80 Gordon Fee, *God's Empowering Presence* (Hendrickson, 1994) p 806.

young people, but I believe the key issues to be the refusal of a strategy of protection, a commitment to model discipleship and discernment in the world, a Christian community which offers stable relationships, the experience (not just the doctrine) of the assurance of salvation, and a vision of and vocation for God's future kingdom.

Postscript

The cultural transition we are going through is so substantial that I do not believe we will always be able to integrate work with young people into our existing church structures and forms of worship. The emerging phenomenon of youth congregations needs to be taken very seriously. I have no belief in a single generation church, but we may be being called to plant the church in the first generation of a new cultural era. The eclectic, pick-and-mix approach to constructing culture should not automatically be seen as negative, and need not be unprincipled. Under the lordship of Christ, it could lead to a renewal of imagination concerning the form of the church. But that is a matter for another book in another series.